American History Writing Prompts

★ • ★

185 Intriguing Historical Facts and Quotations—
With Companion Prompts—That Get Kids Thinking
and Writing About the History You Teach

By Jeannette Sanderson

SCHOLASTIC

PROFESSIONAL BOOKS

New York • Toronto • London • Auckland • Sydney
Mexico City • New Delhi • Hong Kong

Dedicated to all the teachers who make
history come alive for their students.

Cover design by Jaime Lucero
Cover photographs from the Library of Congress
Cover art by Mona Mark
Interior design by Sydney Wright
Interior photographs: New York Public Library, pp. 17, 20, 21, and 30; Granger Collection, p. 13; International Portrait
Gallery, p. 12; International Museum of Photography at George Eastman House, p. 42; Woolaroc Museum, p. 9; AP Wide
World, pp. 15 and 38; Western History Collections, University of Oklahoma Library, p. 28; Union Pacific Railroad, p. 29.
All other photos, Library of Congress.

ISBN: 0-439-04094-9

Printed in the U.S.A.

Table of Contents

Introduction

"If men could learn from history, what lessons it might teach us!"

—Samuel Taylor Coleridge (1772-1834)

There's no doubt about the importance of learning history. The question is, what is the best way to teach it?

When I was young, I thought history was boring. It was a bunch of dates and facts to be memorized just long enough to pass a history test and then be forgotten. Why all the fuss about something as dry as the dust on my history book jacket, I wondered. Then, suddenly, everything changed. I don't remember if it was a good teacher or a good book that made history come alive for me, but I will be forever grateful for having my eyes opened. I no longer see history as the story of the dead but rather as the story of the living. The people we learn about may be dead now but were very much alive in the past.

Good teachers make history come alive. They make us care about the people who lived before us. They encourage us to use our imaginations to walk in the footsteps of those who came before us. With good teaching, dates and places are not so much facts to memorize as markers along a journey, the human journey.

I have also learned that history is about the living in another way—history is written by the living. And, like any story, "his" story may not be "her" story, so it is good to try to look at the story from all sides. The person with the loudest voice—or the busiest printing press—is not necessarily telling the truth, or at least the whole truth. He is only telling "his" story.

Because I have grown to love history, all the stories in the human journey, I was very excited when my editor asked me to write this book. I would have a chance to explore American history all over again. But more than that, I would have the chance to help make history come alive for children. I could do for others what was done for me.

The first question I asked myself when researching and writing this book was, Is this something teachers teach? I think you'll find the answer is yes. The writing prompts cover all of American history—from the artifacts left by the first Americans to the Persian Gulf War and everything in between. To help you zero in on the period your class is studying, the writing prompts are divided into 15 sections. You can read each section in full to find topics of special interest to you or you can skim and use the boldfaced writing prompt subheads as your guide to quickly find a topic to write about. Depending on interest and skill level, among other things, you can ask students to write as much or as little in response to each writing prompt as you wish.

The second question I asked myself when researching and writing this book was, Does this show the different sides to the story? Will these writing prompts help students see that along with the facts there is a lot of fiction in history? I think the answer to this question is also yes.

The third and final question I asked myself when writing this book was, Will this help make history come alive for students? I hope you and your students find the answer to this question to be a resounding yes.

The First Americans

★ History in Artifacts ★

Much of what historians have learned about how the first Americans lived is based on artifacts, or the objects they left behind.

Pick a single object from your room at home. Imagine someone finding it thousands of years from now. Write as if you were that person. Describe the object, what you think it is and what it was used for, and write what you think the object tells about the person who owned it.

★ Columbus's "Discovery" ★

In a letter dated February 15, 1493, Christopher Columbus wrote: "I discovered a great many islands, inhabited by numberless people; and of all I have taken possession for their Highnesses by proclamation and display of the Royal Standard without opposition."

Do you think Columbus had the right to take possession of the islands he "discovered"? Why do you think he was able to do so without opposition? Do you think people can make any kind of fair deal when they don't understand each other's language? Explain.

★ Celebrating Columbus Day ★

On October 12, Americans celebrate Columbus Day, in honor of Columbus's discovery of America.

Write a paragraph about Columbus Day celebrations from the perspective of a Native American.

★ Indians or Native ★ Americans?

Five hundred years ago Christopher Columbus, thinking he had reached India, called Native Americans Indians. We also call the first people to settle America Native Americans.

Do you think it makes a difference whether we use the name Indians or Native Americans? Tell why or why not.

★ Native American Foods ★

Food is one of the many areas in which Native Americans have made significant contributions to American culture. Potatoes, sweet potatoes, corn, tomatoes, beans, turkey, maple sugar, vanilla, and cacao (used to make chocolate) were all Native American staples. Today, many of these foods are important to our Thanksgiving feasts.

Imagine a Thanksgiving dinner without any of these foods. Write how you would feel if none of these foods were placed on your Thanksgiving table.

★ Horses Are Brought to ★ America

When Spanish explorer Hernando de Soto landed in Florida in 1539, he brought with him something Native Americans of that time had never seen before—horses. (Although native to North America, horses had disappeared here by about 8000 B.C.)

Imagine you are a Native American seeing a horse—with a person atop it—for the first time. Describe what you see. Write how it makes you feel.

★ The Purchase of ★ Manhattan Island

In 1624, Dutchman Peter Minuit bought the island of Manhattan from the Manhattan Indians for trinkets worth 60 gelders (calculated to be worth about $24 by a 19th-century historian). The Indians probably thought they were getting a great deal because, to most Native Americans, land—like the air you breathe—was not something you could own. So to the Manhattan Indians, the Dutch were giving them money simply because an island bore their name.

In the end, who do you think got the best deal in the 1624 trade, the Dutch or the Manhattan Indians? Explain.

★ Native Americans ★ and the Law

On June 11, 1675, a New England farmer killed a Native American who was stealing his cattle. The local Indian chief, Metacomet (1639?–1676), protested the murder to local white leaders. When they ignored Metacomet's complaints, he took justice into his own hands and murdered the farmer, his father, and five other settlers.

How do you think local white leaders should have responded to Metacomet? Were they right to ignore him? Do you think Metacomet was right to take matters into his own hands? Explain why or why not.

★ King Philip's War ★

King Philip's War (1675–1676) was fought between New Englanders and the Wampanoags, Narragansetts, and the

Nipmucks. The costly war was sparked by a New England farmer's murder of an Indian he found stealing his cattle. But the spark had received ample kindling—the New England colonists' desire for more and more land, their growing population, and the way they looked down on the local Wampanoag chief, Metacomet (1639?–1676), whom the English mockingly called King Philip.

Imagine a stranger moving—uninvited—into your home, using more and more of your things, inviting his family and friends to join him, and treating you with disrespect in the bargain. How would that make you feel? What would you do in such a situation? How does this compare to the situation of Native Americans who lived in New England in the late 17th century?

★ The Indian Removal Act ★ of 1830

President Andrew Jackson (1767–1845) believed that the only way to end the fighting between whites and Native Americans was to "remove" all Indians from lands east of the Mississippi. To this end, he helped pass the Indian Removal Act of 1830. This law evicted major Indian tribes from land east of the Mississippi and sent them to "Indian Territory," in the West. To the Indians, who were reluctant to move, he said, "Young chiefs, forget the prejudices [attachment] you feel for the soil of your birth."

Do you think the United States government had the right to tell Native Americans to move? Explain why or why not. What do you think of President Jackson's suggestion that Native Americans ignore their attachment to their homeland? How do you think you would have felt upon receiving such a request? What do you think you would have done?

★ The Indian Removal Act ★ of 1830

When informing the Creek Indians of Alabama and Florida of the Indian Removal Act of 1830, President Andrew Jackson (1767–1845) wrote: "Friends and brothers, listen. Where you are now, you and my white children are too near each other to live in harmony and peace . . . . Beyond the great river Mississippi . . . your white brothers will not trouble you . . . and you can live there as long as the grass grows or the water runs, in peace and plenty."

How are President Jackson's words representative of many of the promises the United States government made to Native Americans, and then broke? There is a saying that promises are meant to be broken. Do you agree? Has someone ever broken a promise to you? How did it make you feel? Do you think there is ever a good reason to break a promise?

★ The Trail of Tears ★

Beginning in the fall of 1838, the Cherokee Indians were marched under armed escort from their homeland in Georgia through Tennessee and Kentucky, across the Ohio and Missouri rivers, and into Indian Territory and what would later become Oklahoma. Cold, hungry, and abused by their military guards, about 4,000 Cherokees died during the march. The Cherokees came to call this 1,200-mile journey the "Trail of Tears."

Imagine you hear the words Trail of Tears, but you know nothing about the Cherokees' journey. Describe what you imagine a journey with such a name would be like.

★ The Trail of Tears ★

A Georgia soldier who accompanied the Cherokee Indians on the Trail of Tears recalled the journey many years later: "I fought through the Civil War and have seen men shot to pieces and slaughtered by thousands, but the Cherokee removal was the cruelest work I ever saw."

Look up the definition of the word cruel. How does it apply to the Cherokee removal?

What other event in American history would you describe as cruel? Explain.

★ The Treaty of 1868 ★

The Black Hills of Dakota are sacred to the Sioux Indians. In an 1868 treaty, the United States recognized the Black Hills as part of the Great Sioux Reservation and set them aside for exclusive use by the Sioux people. But when gold was discovered there in 1874, the government wanted the Indians off the land. First they tried to persuade the Sioux to sell or lease the land. The Sioux refused. So the government ordered them off the land, and war erupted.

The dictionary defines bully as "one who is cruel to others weaker than himself." Who was the bully in this situation? Explain your answer. Has anyone ever tried to bully you? Were you able to stop it? If so, how? If not, why not?

★ The Battle of Little Bighorn ★

In a major victory, the Sioux defeated General George Armstrong Custer (1839–1876) at the Battle of Little Bighorn in

1876. A Sioux warrior later described this as a "hollow victory." Why did he use these words? Within little more than a year, the Sioux Indians were driven off their land and onto reservations.

What do you think the Sioux warrior meant by "hollow victory"? Have you ever had a hollow victory? Explain.

★ Buffalo and the Indians ★

Many Indians relied on the millions of buffalo that once roamed the Great Plains for their survival, and they made the most of these great mammals. They made clothing, moccasins, tepees, furniture, and drums, among other things, from buffalo hides. They ate buffalo meat and used it in religious ceremonies. They made food, paint, and cosmetics from buffalo fat and marrow. They used buffalo fur ceremonially and to make rope. They used buffalo hoofs ceremonially and to make tools and glue. They used the buffalo's bladder as a storage pouch. They even used buffalo dung as fuel.

What can we learn about conservation from the way the Great Plains Indians made use of the buffalo? Brainstorm a list of ways you can conserve natural resources. Choose one and write an essay trying to persuade others how and why they should adopt the conservation measures you suggest.

★ Indian Surrender ★

Upon surrendering to the United States Army in 1890, Chief Joseph the Younger (1840–1904) of the Nez Perce Indians spoke the following words:

". . . Hear me, my chiefs! I am tired; my heart is sick and sad. From where the sun now stands, I will fight no more forever."

Imagine you are a Nez Perce Indian. Write a paragraph explaining how you would feel after hearing these words. Then imagine you are a U.S. soldier who has been fighting against the Nez Perce Indians. Write a paragraph explaining how you would feel after hearing Chief Joseph's words.

Exploration and Colonization

★ New Worlds ★

It has been said that one reason an age of exploration began in the 15th century was that Spain and England needed a new world. They needed more land for their growing populations and more markets for their products.

What is left to explore in the 21st century? How does this new world compare to the one the Europeans explored more than 500 years ago?

★ A New Route to the Far East ★

The Far East was an important trading destination for Europeans in the 15th century. Many people considered the spices found there to be as valuable as gold, because spices helped preserve food. (This was very important, since refrigeration had not yet been invented.) In the late 1400s, Italian sailor Christopher Columbus (1451–1506) proposed that by sailing west he could reach the Far East faster and more easily than the traders traveling on land could. He presented his proposal to the kings of Portugal, England, France, and Spain in the hopes of getting one of these governments to sponsor such a voyage.

Imagine you are Christopher Columbus meeting with a European ruler regarding the westward journey you want to make to the Far East. Write the argument you would use to convince the ruler that he or she should finance your journey.

★ Christopher Columbus's ★ Journey

Italian sailor Christopher Columbus (1451–1506) set sail from Palos, Spain, on August 3, 1492, on what he thought would be a 3,000-mile journey to China. When his ships failed to reach land

by late September, Columbus realized the Far East must be farther away than he had calculated. Afraid to further upset his already-frightened sailors—some of whom believed the earth was flat and feared sailing right off the edge of it—Columbus

began keeping two log books. In one, which he kept to himself, Columbus accurately recorded the distance traveled. In another, which he showed to his crew, Columbus made it appear that the ships hadn't traveled nearly as far as they had.

Do you think Columbus was right to deceive his crew regarding the distance they had traveled? Justify your reasoning. Has someone ever deceived you to get you to act in a certain way? (For example, maybe one of your parents told you it was later than it was to get you to move faster in the morning.) Did the deceit work? How did it make you feel?

★ The New World Gets a Name ★

Christopher Columbus (1451–1506) didn't have the honor of having the land he "discovered" named after him; that honor went to a later explorer, Amerigo Vespucci (1454–1512). In 1507, an atlas came out with a map using a version of Vespucci's first name to label the land he had explored.

Imagine you're one of Columbus's children reading the new atlas. How would you feel when you saw that America had been named, not after your father, but after Amerigo Vespucci? Write a letter telling the atlas's author how you feel. (Are you angry? Do you want the name changed? Do you want another place or landmark named after your father?)

★ The Fountain of Youth ★

Spanish explorer Juan Ponce de Leon (1460–1521) was the first European to set foot on what would become United States soil. He went to Florida in 1513 in search of a fabled fountain of youth.

Imagine if Ponce de Leon had found a fountain of youth in Florida. How would our world be different if such a fountain existed? Do you think it would be better or worse? Explain why or why not.

★ "Send Me Some Gold" ★

When Montezuma II, ruler of the Aztecs, gave Spanish conquistador Hernan Cortes (1485–1547) gems and gold, Cortes said: "Send me some more . . . because I and my companions suffer from a disease of the heart which can be cured only with gold."

Think of at least one way greed has helped shape the United States and write about it. (Consider the conquistadors, slavery, the gold rush, and the role of big business in U.S. history, among other things.)

★ Native Americans: ★ Slaves or Converts

The Spanish conquistadors wanted to enslave the Native Americans they

encountered in the New World; the Spanish missionaries wanted to convert the Native Americans to Christianity.

Do you think people from one culture have the right to impose their way of life on people from another culture? Explain.

★ The Lost Colony of Roanoke ★

In 1587, Sir Walter Raleigh sent three ships and 117 men, women, and children to establish a colony at Roanoke Island in what is now North Carolina. Shortly after the colonists arrived, their leader, John White,

sailed back to England for much-needed supplies. He left behind his daughter Eleanor Dare and his granddaughter Virginia Dare, the first English child born in the New World. But England's war with Spain prevented White from returning to Roanoke until 1590. When he did finally return to the island, there was no trace of the settlers and barely a trace of the settlement. "Croatoan," the name of a nearby island, was carved onto a tree. White tried to sail to Croatoan, but bad weather blew his ship off course.

No one knows what happened to the "lost colony" on Roanoke Island.

Imagine you are John White and you have just returned to Roanoke Island in 1590. Write your journal entry for that day.

★ The Lost Colony of Roanoke ★

The fate of the "lost colony" of Roanoke Island (see above) continues to be a mystery. There are theories that the colonists died of disease, starved to death, were killed by hostile Indians, or moved to Croatoan or elsewhere.

Write a one-page essay telling what you imagine happened to the "lost colony."

★ Fair Trades ★

English and French traders gave Native Americans liquor in exchange for furs and other goods they wanted. Many missionaries argued against this, saying it was wrong to introduce alcohol to Native Americans. The traders argued back that the Native Americans could make their own choices.

Who do you agree with, the missionaries or the traders? How could your argument be applied to the sale of such substances as alcohol and tobacco today?

★ The Black Legend ★

Spanish colonial government from the 16th to the 18th centuries was dominated by the

encomienda system. An *encomendar* was a type of deed given to colonists by the Spanish crown. The deed gave the colonists specific tracts of land as well as the right to use the native people living on that land as laborers. A "Black Legend" grew up around Spain and the New World partly because of the cruel way in which many of the *encomenderos* treated their laborers.

Think of slavery and how it compares to the encomienda system. Why do you think so many people have been oppressed throughout history in the United States and elsewhere? Do you think the need to oppress is part of human nature? What do you think can be done about it?

★ Jamestown ★

Jamestown, settled in 1607, became the first permanent English settlement in the New World. In the settlement's early years, however, its future looked about as promising as Roanoke's. More than half of the original 144 colonists died within the first year. Many died from disease or were killed by Indians, but most died of starvation. The problem was that most of the colonists were gentlemen and weren't used to the hard physical labor a colony needed to survive. When he took over Jamestown in 1608, Captain John Smith (1580–1631) put all of the colonists, regardless of class, to work. When some complained that they were gentlemen and could not farm or clear land, Smith told them, "He that will not work shall not eat."

Do you think that John Smith was fair to insist that all colonists work? Do you think such a rule as "He that will not work shall not eat" could or should be put into effect in today's society? Explain why or why not.

★ Pocahontas Saves ★ Captain John Smith

Captain John Smith (1580–1631) was captured by the Powhatan Indians in 1607 and sentenced to death. Pocahontas (1595–1617) begged her father, Chief Powhatan (1550?–1618), to spare Smith's life. Powhatan refused, and Smith was laid out with his head on stones to be clubbed to death. Pocahontas quickly put Captain Smith's head in her arms and rested her own head on his. In this way, Pocahontas saved John Smith's life.

Describe a situation in which you might save the life of a total stranger.

★ Taking by Force ★

In 1607, Chief Powhatan (1550?–1618) of the Powhatan Indians said to English Captain John Smith (1580–1631), "Why will you take by force what you may have quietly by love?"

What did Chief Powhatan mean by that statement? When, if ever, is it necessary to use force to get what you want?

★ Tobacco: Saving Crop or ★ Stinking Weed

Tobacco saved the Jamestown colony. In 1612, when English settler John Rolfe (1585–1622) crossed Virginia tobacco with a milder Jamaican leaf, he created a tobacco that the English went wild for. He also created Virginia's first cash crop, and secured her future. But even back then, tobacco was a questionable commodity. England's King James I (1566–1625) hated the plant and called tobacco the "stinking weed." He said it was "hateful to the nose, harmful to the brain, and dangerous to the lungs."

Should the colonists in Virginia have continued to grow tobacco even though they were aware of its questionable effects on health? Explain. How does the situation in 17th-century Jamestown compare to that of poor farmers in some countries today who, struggling to make a living, grow coca, used to make cocaine, and other drugs?

★ The Indians Fight Back ★

The Powhatan Indians grew increasingly alarmed as English settlers took more and more land. In an effort to stop the growth, the Powhatans attacked the Jamestown colony in 1622 and killed nearly 350 settlers. One colonist later wrote of the Indians, "Either we must clear them or they us out of the country."

What do you think of the colonist's statement? Do you think it would have been possible for the colonists and the Indians to live together peacefully? If so, how? If not, why not?

★ The Pilgrims Sail to the ★ New World

The Pilgrims came to the New World in search of religious freedom. They sailed from Plymouth, England, on September 16, 1620, and didn't sight land until November 19 of that year. They thanked God when they saw the land (the tip of Cape Cod). But all of their emotions weren't positive ones. Future Plymouth Colony governor William Bradford (1590–1657) wrote of their sighting:

"They had now no friends to welcome them, no inns to . . . refresh their weather-beaten bodies . . . . Besides, what could they see but a hideous and desolate wilderness, full of wild beasts and wild men?"

Would you make the same kind of journey the Pilgrims did to find religious freedom? Are there any freedoms that would move you to make a similar journey? Explain.

★ The *Mayflower* Compact ★

When the Pilgrims landed off Cape Cod in November 1620, they found themselves in a bind: They were landing in a "lawless" place. (The Virginia Company, which had financed their journey, had no power that far north.) Fearing that the colony wouldn't survive without laws, the Pilgrims drew up an agreement before setting foot on land. Under this agreement, the Pilgrims promised to set up a government that would make "just and equal laws" for the good of the colony.

Imagine you are one of the first leaders of Plymouth Colony. Write what you think would be "just and equal laws" for the good of your colony.

★ First Thanksgiving ★

In the fall of 1621, the Pilgrims had a feast to celebrate their first harvest. They invited the neighboring Wampanoag Indians who, by helping them plant crops and build homes, had helped them survive the first winter. The Pilgrims thanked these Native Americans and God for their good harvest with a Thanksgiving feast.

Think of what you have to be thankful for. Imagine having a thanksgiving feast to show your thanks. Write a plan for such a feast. When and where would it be? Who would you invite? What would you serve? Would you have any special words for your guests? Then ask yourself, what are some actual ways I can show my thanks?

★ The Puritans ★

When John Winthrop (1588–1649) was elected the first governor of the Massachusetts Bay Colony, he told his fellow Puritan settlers what he expected of them: "We shall be as a city upon a hill. The eyes of all people are upon us."

What do you think Winthrop was asking of the Puritan settlers? Has anyone ever asked you to set a good example? How important do you think setting a good example is in teaching proper behavior?

★ Reverend Roger Williams ★

When Reverend Roger Williams (1603?–1683) emigrated from England to Boston in 1631, his views quickly upset Puritan rulers there. One of his controversial beliefs was that the lands chartered to the Massachusetts Bay and Plymouth colonies actually belonged to the Native Americans who lived there; another was that a civil government should not enforce religious laws, which the Massachusetts Bay government did. The Massachusetts General Court ordered Williams to change his views. He refused, and was expelled from the Massachusetts Bay Colony. In 1636, Williams purchased a small plot of land from the Indians of Narragansett Bay and established Providence, the first settlement in Rhode Island.

Imagine you are a conservative Puritan minister preaching in 1635. Write a short sermon about the mistaken beliefs of

Reverend Roger Williams. Then imagine you are Roger Williams and write a short rebuttal to the minister's charges.

★ Anne Hutchinson ★

Anne Hutchinson (1591–1643) was a member of the Massachusetts Bay Colony who publicly discussed what she believed to be faults with Puritan ways. This upset Puritan ministers. In 1637, they had Hutchinson brought to trial, where she was found guilty and banished from the colony.

Before the Puritans came to the New World, many were forced out of England because of their religious beliefs. How is it ironic, then, that Anne Hutchinson was forced out of Massachusetts Bay Colony for her religious beliefs?

★ The Salem Witch Trials ★

By the end of 1692, 140 people in Salem, Massachusetts, had been accused of witchcraft. Most of the accused were poor, elderly women who did not get along with their neighbors.

What does the description of the accused tell you about the Salem witch trials? Do you think such a situation could arise in this day and age? Explain your thinking.

★ William Penn and the ★ Quakers

One of the main reasons William Penn (1644–1718) founded Pennsylvania in 1682 was to allow the Society of Friends, or Quakers, a place to worship. Among the Quakers' religious beliefs was that all killing was wrong. This meant that they would not serve in the military or pay taxes that supported the military.

Do you think a person's religious beliefs should allow him or her to be excused from such things as serving in the military or paying taxes? Tell why or why not.

The Road to Independence

★ Freedom of the Press ★

In 1734, New York Weekly Journal editor John Peter Zenger (1697–1746) printed articles that attacked the administration of New York governor William Crosby. This prompted Crosby to shut down the paper and jail Zenger. Philadelphia lawyer Alexander Hamilton (1755–1804) defended Zenger at his trial. Hamilton said that people had the right to criticize their leaders, as long as what they wrote was true. The jury agreed and found Zenger not guilty. Hamilton later said, "You have laid a noble foundation for securing to ourselves that to which Nature and the Laws of our country have given us a Right—the Liberty—both of exposing and opposing arbitrary Power by speaking and writing Truth."

Take advantage of this freedom—freedom of the press. Write a letter to the editor of a newspaper or magazine about something that concerns you.

★ Wit and Wisdom ★

Benjamin Franklin (1706–1790) wrote and published Poor Richard's Almanac in 18th-century Philadelphia. Here are some proverbs, or sayings, from that publication:

Better slip with foot than tongue.

Haste makes waste.

He that lives upon hope will die fasting.

No gains without pains.

Three may keep a secret, if two of them are dead.

Think about what each of these proverbs means. Choose one that has importance in your own life. Write what it means, and how you relate to it.

★ Mother Country ★

Benjamin Franklin (1706–1790) wrote the following poem about America's relationship with England:

We have an old mother that
   peevish is grown;
She snubs us like children that
   scarce walk alone;
She forgets we're grown up and
   have sense of our own.

What is Franklin saying in this poem? Have you ever felt this way in your own life? Explain.

★ Liberty or Death! ★

After attending the first Continental Congress in Philadelphia, Patrick Henry (1736–1799) returned to the Virginia House of Burgesses and spoke about America's quarrel with England: "Is life so dear or peace so sweet as to be purchased at the price of chains and slavery? I know not what course others may take, but as for me, give me liberty or give me death!"

Imagine you are a member of the Virginia House of Burgesses who has been undecided about what course to take in regard to relations with England. How do you think Patrick Henry's speech might affect you?

★ Taxation Without ★ Representation: The Sugar Act

The English Parliament passed the Sugar Act in 1764 to help pay the huge debt brought about by the French and Indian War. The law required American colonists to pay heavy taxes on sugar, molasses, coffee, wine, and other popular goods imported into the colonies. The English government thought it only fair that the colonists help pay for a war fought on their soil. The colonists strongly disagreed. "No taxation without representation" became a popular political slogan. James Otis

(1725–1783), a radical leader in Massachusetts, wrote that everyone should be "free from all taxes but what he consents to in person or by his representative."

Do you agree with the British government or the colonists regarding the Sugar Act? Why? How much say do you think people should have in how, how much, and why they are taxed?

★ The Stamp Act ★

The Stamp Act, passed by the English Parliament in 1765, required that colonists buy stamps from royally appointed colonial stamp agents for all printed matter—from newspapers to legal documents to playing cards. Riots broke out. The home of Massachusetts governor Thomas Hutchinson was destroyed; the house of a New York stamp agent was ransacked. There was a widespread boycott of the stamps followed by a general boycott of English goods.

Think of the ways in which the colonists protested the Stamp Act. Do you think violence is necessary for protest to be heeded? Do you think nonviolent protest can be successful? Explain. Also, what have you protested in your life? What method(s) have you used? What methods of protest work best for you?

★ The Quartering Act ★

The Quartering Act, passed by Parliament in 1765 and extended several times over

the following decade, required colonial governments to feed and shelter royal troops at colonists' expense, sometimes in the colonists' own homes.

Imagine you are an 18th-century American colonist and you have just been told you must house a British soldier in your home or face possible arrest. How would you feel about it? How would you feel about the government that was forcing you to take such action? What do you think you would do?

★ The Boston Massacre ★

On March 5, 1770, a crowd of Boston protesters began taunting a small group of British soldiers. They started throwing rocks, snow, and ice at the Redcoats. The soldiers grew nervous. When someone yelled "Fire!" (no one knows who), the soldiers fired their guns into the crowd, mortally wounding five people.

Do you think the soldiers were right or wrong to shoot into the crowd? What do you think they should have done? Have you ever been in a situation where you felt threatened? What did you do?

★ The Boston Massacre ★ and John Adams

John Adams (1735–1826), a strong supporter of liberty, believed the British soldiers involved in the Boston Massacre had the right to a fair trial. This was an unpopular belief, but John Adams defended the soldiers nonetheless.

Do you agree that the British soldiers involved in the Boston Massacre had the right to a fair trial? Would you have been willing to take the unpopular position of defending them in court? Explain why or why not.

★ Committees ★ of Correspondence

Committees of correspondence wrote letters throughout the Colonies urging support of patriot causes such as the boycott of English tea to protest the tax on tea.

Imagine you are on a committee of correspondence. Write a letter to people in other colonies asking them to support a tea boycott.

★ The Boston Tea Party ★

The colonists loved tea, but they were less than thrilled with British taxes on their favorite drink. When Parliament passed the Tea Act of May 10, 1773, which allowed the East India Company to undersell American merchants, the colonists were outraged. When three East India Company ships laden with tea arrived in Boston Harbor in November of that year, the colonists refused to let them land and insisted the ships be sent back to England. After learning that Massachusetts governor Thomas Hutchinson (1711–1780) had refused their demands, the patriots took matters into their own hands. On the night of December 16, 1773, a group of patriots disguised as Indians boarded the three ships and dumped all the tea—45 tons of it—into Boston Harbor. The patriots did not harm the ships' crews, the ships themselves, or any other cargo aboard the ships.

Imagine you're one of the people involved or effected by the Boston Tea Party—a patriot, Governor Hutchinson, a member of Parliament, one of the ship's captains, or the owner of the tea. How do you think you would feel the morning after the "tea party"? What do you think you would do?

★ The Boston Tea Party ★

After the Boston Tea Party, England's King George (1738–1820) said, "The die is now cast. The colonies must either submit or triumph."

Explain what you think King George meant by this statement.

★ The Intolerable Acts ★

In response to the Boston Tea Party, an angry British Parliament passed the Coercive Acts. The Intolerable Acts, as the colonists called them, closed Boston harbor until Boston paid for the destroyed tea, and banned, among other things, town meetings not specifically required by law or approved by the governor. Although these acts were meant to punish Boston and stamp out rebellion in the colonies, it had the opposite effect, and led the colonists to convene the First Continental Congress.

Why do you think the Intolerable Acts fueled rather than put out the flames of rebellion? Think of a time when you tried to punish someone and your punishment backfired or when you were punished and your punishment had the opposite effect. Why did the punishment backfire?

★ The First Continental ★ Congress

The First Continental Congress met in Philadelphia in the fall of 1774. There was a nearly equal number of radicals and conservatives at the meetings. The radicals supported the Massachusetts delegation's Suffolk Resolves. These called for people to arm, to disobey the Intolerable Acts, and to collect their own taxes. The conservatives favored a compromise that would maintain ties with England.

Imagine you are a representative at the First Continental Congress. Write a short speech in support of the radical or conservative stand.

★ The First Shot ★

British General Thomas Gage (1721–1787) decided the best way to avoid a fight with the colonists was to take away their weapons. He set out on April 18, 1775, with 700 British troops to capture a rebel arsenal in Concord, Massachusetts. The British were met the next morning on the

Lexington village green by a small force of colonial minutemen. The first shot of the war was fired there, and several minutemen were killed.

The first shot fired at Lexington became known as "the shot heard round the world." Why do you think it became known as this?

★ Loyalists Versus Patriots ★

Not every colonist was a patriot. In fact, historians believe that for every two colonists who supported the war, there was one loyalist who did not.

Imagine you are a loyalist at the start of the American Revolution. What would you do? Would you stay in the colonies or would you move to Canada or to Britain?

★ The Declaration of ★ Independence

In the Declaration of Independence, John Hancock (1737–1793) listed the inalienable rights of humankind as life, liberty, and the pursuit of happiness. Inalienable rights are rights that can't be surrendered or taken away.

Do you believe people have certain inalienable rights? If so, what do you think they are?

★ Join or Die ★

At the signing of the Declaration of Independence on July 4, 1776, Benjamin Franklin (1706–1790) said to John Hancock (1737–1793), "We must indeed all hang together, or, most assuredly, we shall all hang separately."

What did Franklin mean by this remark? When do you think it's important to stick together?

★ Common Sense ★

In his book titled *Common Sense*, Philadelphia patriot Thomas Paine (1737–1809) wrote, "These are the times that try men's souls."

What do you think Thomas Paine meant by those words?

★ Nathan Hale ★

When the British captured Nathan Hale (1755–1776), who was spying for the colonists, they ordered him executed.

These are the words Hale spoke before he was hanged, "I only regret that I have but one life to lose for my country."

Can you imagine giving up your life for your country? If so, give an example of what might lead you to make such a sacrifice. If not, explain why.

A New Nation

★ "From Many, One" ★

The Great Seal of the United States of America shows an eagle with a ribbon in its beak. The Latin words on the ribbon are *e pluribus unum*, which mean "from many, one." This motto, adopted in 1782, tells what the Founding Fathers were trying to do: make a single nation from several states and many individuals.

Do you think the Founding Fathers faced an easy or difficult task in trying to form one nation from several states and many individuals? Explain your answer.

★ The Constitutional ★ Convention— Checks and Balances

During the Constitutional Convention in 1787, the framers created a system of government with three branches: executive, legislative, and judicial. They created a series of checks and balances for each branch: the Supreme Court and Congress check the powers of the president, the president and Congress check the powers of the Supreme Court, and the president and the Supreme Court check the powers of Congress.

Why do you think the framers felt this system of checks and balances was important?

★ The Constitutional ★ Convention— the Great Compromise

When the delegates to the Constitutional Convention were trying to form a new government, there was a great deal of disagreement over how each state should be represented in Congress. Delegates from large states wanted the number of representatives from each state to be based on population. Delegates from smaller states wanted each state to have an equal number of representatives. In the end, Roger Sherman (1721–1793) from Connecticut proposed what has become known as the "Great Compromise." This called for two

houses in the legislature. The upper house, or Senate, would give each state equal representation; the lower house, or House of Representatives, would allow representation based on a state's population.

Imagine you're a delegate at the Constitutional Convention. Write a speech in favor of equal representation, proportional representation, or the so-called Great Compromise.

★ The Constitutional ★ Convention— the Electoral College

The Electoral College—the roundabout way we elect our president—was created because the framers of the Constitution did not want to let the people directly elect the president.

Do you think ordinary people are capable of electing good leaders? Give reasons to explain your answer.

★ The Constitutional ★ Convention— the Three-Fifths Compromise

There was a great deal of debate about whether or not slaves should be counted as part of the population  when apportioning representation in the House of Representatives. Southern states wanted slaves counted, northern states did not. In the end, the framers reached an unusual compromise: They decided to count slaves as three-fifths of a person when deciding the number of representatives from each state and when calculating a state's tax bill.

What do you think of this compromise? If you had been one of the framers, what might you have proposed?

★ Big Versus Small Government ★

Two members of the cabinet of George Washington (1732–1799) had very different ideas about the role of the federal government. Alexander Hamilton (1755–1804), Secretary of the Treasury, wanted a powerful and active federal government. Secretary of State Thomas Jefferson (1743–1826), on the other hand, wanted a weaker central government that left more power in the hands of individuals and states. This fundamental disagreement between these two men gave birth to America's two-party political system.

Do you think the federal government should be powerful and active, as Hamilton wanted, or weaker, to allow more power to states and individuals, as Jefferson wanted? How does your ideal type of federal government compare with what we actually have?

★ Nullification ★

Thomas Jefferson (1743–1826) believed that each state had the right to judge whether or not laws passed by Congress were constitutional. If the state believed they were not, it could *nullify*, or override, the laws, and refuse to obey them.

What do you think would happen if states were allowed to nullify federal laws? What kind of federal government would we have?

★ The Bill of Rights ★

The Bill of Rights, which is the first 10 amendments to the Constitution, was ratified on December 15, 1791. These amendments guarantee citizens a set of inalienable individual rights. They are:

First Amendment: freedom of speech, press, religion, and assembly

Second Amendment: the right to bear arms

Third Amendment: no requirement to quarter troops in peacetime

Fourth Amendment: no unreasonable searches and seizures

Fifth Amendment: no arrest without a grand jury indictment; no double jeopardy; no taking of life, liberty, or property without due process of law or of private property for public use without just compensation

Sixth Amendment: the right to a speedy trial and the right to counsel

Seventh Amendment: the right to a trial by jury

Eighth Amendment: no excessive bail or fines; no cruel or unusual punishment

Ninth Amendment: the rights of the people not to be limited to those given

Tenth Amendment: All powers not delegated to the federal government are reserved to the states, or to the people

Choose one amendment or one freedom from the Bill of Rights and write why it is important to you. Provide at least one example of how it affects your life and what your life would be like without it.

★ "The Star-Spangled Banner" ★

Francis Scott Key (1779–1843) wrote "The Star-Spangled Banner" on September 14, 1814. He had been detained on a British warship and watched through the night as the British bombarded Fort McHenry in Baltimore Harbor. Here are the words Key wrote for the poem that eventually became our national anthem:

Oh, say! can you see, by the dawn's early
    light,
What so proudly we hailed at the twilight's
    last gleaming?
Whose broad stripes and bright stars,
    through the perilous fight,
O'er the ramparts we watched were so
    gallantly streaming?
And the rockets' red glare, the bombs
    bursting in air,
Gave proof through the night, that our flag
    was still there.
O, say, does that Star Spangled Banner yet
    wave

O'er the land of the free and the home of the brave?

Write how you think Key felt when he wrote this poem. Write a poem about something that makes you feel proud of this country.

★ The Erie Canal ★

New York governor DeWitt Clinton (1769–1828) was laughed at when he first proposed building a 363-mile-long canal to connect the Hudson River and the Great Lakes. Most canals at the time were just a few miles long. Even Thomas Jefferson (1743–1826), always a man ahead of his time, thought Clinton was out of his mind to want to undertake such a project. "It is a splendid project that may be executed a century hence," Jefferson said. "But it is little short of madness to think of it at this day." Clinton refused to be discouraged, however, and broke ground on "Clinton's Ditch," as his opponents called it, on July 4, 1817. The Erie Canal, as it came to be called, took eight years to build, but it was an instant success.

Have you ever been told you would be unable to do something but went ahead and did it anyway, against the odds? How did you do it? What kind of person do you think it takes to beat the odds in this way?

★ Girls and Factories ★

Francis Cabot Lowell built our nation's first cotton factory in Waltham, Massachusetts, in 1813. Unable to find enough men to work his mills, Lowell decided to hire farm girls to do the work. Not only was there a plentiful supply of such labor, but it came cheap: Lowell only had to pay the girls half of what he would have had to pay men.

Just because Lowell could pay the girls half as much as men for the same work, do you think he should have? Or do you think he should have paid the girls what he would have paid men for the same work? Have you ever received less pay for your work because of your age? Do you think that was right? Tell why or why not.

★ Spinning Wheel to Factory ★

Before the mass production of factories, most families worked at home. But cotton factories made home spinning and weaving a thing of the past. Factories changed the way people worked and lived. By the mid-1800s, many people worked in factories; some even lived in factory boarding houses.

How do you think mass production might have helped the family? How do you think it might have harmed it?

★ Manifest Destiny ★

New York Post editor John O'Sullivan wrote in 1845, "It is our manifest destiny to overspread and to possess the whole of the continent which Providence has given us."

What do you think O'Sullivan meant by the words "manifest destiny"? How do you think these words would have made a settler feel? How do you think they would have made a Native American feel?

★ Westward Ho! ★

Many settlers made long, hard journeys in search of a better life in the west. A family on the Oregon Trail might spend six months traversing 2,000 miles in a covered wagon to reach its destination. Such journeys meant dealing with harsh weather and dwindling supplies of food and water. Sometimes they meant Indian attacks,

buffalo stampedes, and prairie fires. Yet thousands of settlers still made this journey to what they hoped was a better life.

What kind of person do you think it took to make—and survive—such a journey? What qualities do you have that you think would have helped you on such a journey?

★ California Gold Rush ★

Gold was discovered in California in 1848, causing thousands of people from all over the world to leave family, friends, and work and travel thousands of miles for the chance to find gold and strike it rich.

Would you leave your home—your family, friends, and school—and travel thousands of miles for the chance to find gold or other riches? Give reasons to support your answers.

★ The Mexican-American War ★

United States citizens had mixed feelings about the Mexican-American War (1846–1848). Many supported our country's efforts to make California and New Mexico—which included present-day Arizona, Utah, and Nevada—part of our growing nation. Others, however, saw the war as an unfair act of aggression on our part.

Imagine you are living in 19th-century America. Write a letter to the editor of your newspaper to support or protest the Mexican-American War.

★ "Civil Disobedience" ★

New England writer Henry David Thoreau (1817–1862) was a strong supporter of individual freedom. He was arrested and spent a day in jail for refusing to pay a poll tax. He could not pay the tax, he argued, because then he would be supporting the crimes of the government, especially the war with Mexico. He later wrote in his essay "Civil Disobedience" (1849), "The only obligation which I have a right to assume is to do at any time what I think is right."

Do you agree with Thoreau that the only obligation any of us has is to do what we think is right? Tell why or why not. What kind of society do you think we would have if we all held firmly to this belief?

★ The Pony Express ★

William H. Russell founded the Pony Express in 1858 as a faster way to deliver mail. He planned to have a relay of horses and riders stretching across the continent. Russell found his riders by advertising for "daring young men, preferably orphans."

Why do you think Russell asked for "daring young men, preferably orphans"? What other kinds of jobs might this advertisement apply to?

★ The Transcontinental ★ Railroad

The final section of the transcontinental railroad, completed in 1869, ran from Nebraska to California, and thus connected the entire United States through steel tracks.

One historian has said that the transcontinental railroad did more than politics to bind East and West into a single nation. How do you think the railroad accomplished that?

★ Western Outlaws ★

Jesse James (1847–1882) was one of many western outlaws who was hailed as a hero as much as he was condemned as a criminal. He robbed big banks and railroads, but many common people saw justice in his actions. After all, they asked, don't big banks and railroads rob us on a daily basis?

Do you think Jesse James and other western outlaws were heroes or criminals for robbing big banks and railroads? Is robbery the best way to get back at organizations you feel are taking advantage of you? What other actions could you take?

Slavery

★ All Men Created Equal? ★

In the Declaration of Independence, Thomas Jefferson (1743–1826) wrote, "All men are created equal." Yet Jefferson, along with George Washington (1732–1799) and many members of Congress, kept slaves.

How do Thomas Jefferson's words and actions show that the Founding Fathers were far from perfect? Do you think we should expect our politicians to be perfect? Just how much should we expect from them?

★ Like Father, Like Son ★

Slaves were first introduced into the colonies in 1619, but it wasn't until 1662 that Virginia passed a law making slavery hereditary. That meant that not only were all black people who were brought into Virginia slaves for life, but their children would also be enslaved for life.

Write how you think a slave would feel upon learning about the new law that made a slave's children slaves.

★ Don't Teach Slaves to Read ★

Most colonies had laws that made it illegal to teach a slave to read or write.

Why do you think such laws were passed? What were slave owners afraid of? How important do you think reading and writing are to a free society, and why?

★ Importing Slaves Becomes ★ Illegal

Congress passed a law outlawing the importation of slaves as of January 1, 1808.

In 1808, there were about one million black slaves in America. What effect, if any, do you think the law against importation had on the institution of slavery in the United States?

★ Missouri: Free or Slave? ★ A Compromise

In 1817, the United States Congress had 22 senators from northern states and 22 senators from southern states. The balance between the nonslaveholding North and the slaveholding South became threatened when Missouri petitioned Congress for admission to the Union as a slaveholding state. Senators from the North were quick to argue that Congress had the right to ban slavery in new states. Senators from the South argued that new states had the right to determine for themselves whether or not they would allow slavery. In 1820, Congress made a compromise, the Missouri Compromise. Under this law, Congress admitted Missouri to the Union as a slave state but declared that all parts of the Louisiana Purchase territory north of Missouri's southern boundary would be forever free.

Do you agree with the senators from the North, who argued that Congress had a right to ban slavery in new states or with the senators from the South, who argued that new states should have the same right as the original 13 states—to determine slaveholding status for themselves? What do you think of the compromise that the senators finally reached?

★ The Missouri Compromise ★ Divides the Country

With the Missouri Compromise of 1820, the United States became clearly divided along strict sectional lines. John Quincy Adams (1767–1848), who would later become president, called the Missouri Compromise, the "title page to a great tragic volume."

What do you think Adams meant by his description of the Missouri Compromise? Do you think the compromise was good or bad for the future of our country?

★ Female Abolitionists ★

Sisters Sarah and Angelina Grimke grew up on a South Carolina plantation surrounded by slaves. But they found slavery horrible, and, when grown, moved north. Soon the Grimke sisters were addressing women about abolition for the American Anti-Slavery Society. They told their audiences, "Women ought to feel a special sympathy for the colored man for, like him, she has been accused of mental inferiority and denied a good education."

Do you agree that women especially should have been sympathetic to the plight of slaves? Do you think groups that are mistreated by society should stand up for one another? Tell why or why not.

★ Frederick Douglass ★

Frederick Douglass (1817–1895), who escaped from slavery in Maryland, opened many people's eyes to the horrors of slavery in his book *Narrative of the Life of Frederick Douglass*, published in 1845. In it, Douglass says that he never saw his father. Of his mother, who worked in the fields from dawn to dusk, he says, "I do not remember ever seeing my mother by the light of day."

Who is the most important and influential family member in your life? How would your life be different if you saw this person as infrequently as Douglass saw his mother?

★ The Fugitive Slave Law ★

The Fugitive Slave Law, passed in 1850, required all United States citizens to help capture and return runaway slaves to their owners.

Imagine living in 1850. Would you have obeyed this law? What if disobeying it meant certain jail or fines for you and, possibly, your family? When, if ever, do you think it is okay to break the law?

★ The Dred Scott Case ★

Dred Scott (1795?–1858) was a slave who had moved with his owner from a slave state to a free territory. When his owner died, Scott said he was a free man, because he lived in a free territory. His owner's widow disagreed. The case went all the way to the Supreme Court, where the majority of justices ruled against Scott. In its 1857 ruling, the Court said, among other things, that Congress had no authority to restrict slavery in the territories, and that the Missouri Compromise was unconstitutional.

Imagine you're a Supreme Court Justice in 1857. Write your opinion of the Dred Scott case. Is Dred Scott a slave or is he free? Give reasons for your opinion.

★ A House Divided ★

On June 17, 1858, Republican lawyer Abraham Lincoln (1809–1865) spoke to a state Republican convention in Springfield, Illinois. Here is part of his speech:

A house divided against itself cannot stand.

I believe this government cannot endure, permanently half slave and half free.

I do not expect the Union to be dissolved; I do not expect the house to fall; but I do expect it will cease to be divided.

What did Lincoln mean when he said, "A house divided against itself cannot stand"? Do you agree? Describe your reasoning. Do you think history showed the truth of Lincoln's words? Explain why or why not.

★ John Brown's Raid ★

New Englander John Brown (1800–1859) was a staunch abolitionist. Some say he was crazy. On October 16, 1859, Brown, along with more than a dozen followers, attacked the federal arsenal at Harper's Ferry, Virginia. He had hoped to use seized weapons to arm slaves for a revolt. But Brown's plan failed, and he and his followers were quickly captured. Brown was tried for treason, convicted, and hanged on December 2, 1859.

To many southerners, Brown was yet another Yankee who wanted to change their way of life. Do you think Brown and other abolitionists had a right to try to change the way people in the South lived and worked? When is it okay to interfere in someone's life? When is it not?

★ Harriet Tubman and the ★ Underground Railroad

The Underground Railroad was the informal system that helped as many as 100,000 escaped slaves reach the Northeast or Canada between 1800 and 1861. As fugitive slaves traveled from one safe spot to another, they were helped by "conductors." Some of these conductors were white abolitionists, others were escaped slaves who returned to help others find their way to freedom. One such conductor was Harriet Tubman (1820–1913), who fled from slavery. Like others, she took great risks each time she returned to the South. Tubman's bravery helped to bring at least 300 slaves, including her parents, to freedom.

Imagine you're a fugitive slave who has found your way North to freedom. Would you risk your freedom, maybe even your life, to return to the South and try to help other people escape as you did? Give reasons for your answer.

The Civil War

★ The Confederacy ★

By February 1861, six states (Alabama, Florida, Georgia, Louisiana, Mississippi, and South Carolina) had seceded from the Union and formed the Confederate States of America. They elected Jefferson Davis (1808–1889), U.S. Senator from Mississippi, as president. According to Davis, Lincoln and other Republicans threatened the liberty, property, and honor of the South.

Write a short acceptance speech that you think Jefferson Davis might have made after his 1861 election.

★ Can the Union and the ★ Confederacy Coexist?

At the time the Confederacy was formed, some northerners believed the Union should just let those southern states go.

What do you think? Do you think the seceding states should have been permit- *ted to leave the Union? What do you think that would have meant to the remaining states? What kind of example do you think it would have set?*

★ Freeing the Slaves Versus ★ Preserving the Union

President Abraham Lincoln (1809–1865) personally hated slavery, but his first priority was to preserve the Union, not to free the slaves. This was clear in his response to journalist and political leader Horace Greeley's public letter demanding that Lincoln free all slaves: "If I could save the Union without freeing *any* slave," Lincoln said, "I would do it; and if I could save it by freeing *all* the slaves, I would do it; and if I could save it by freeing some and leaving others alone, I would also do that . . . I intend no modification of my oft-expressed personal wish that all men everywhere could be free."

Do you think it was easy or difficult for Lincoln to put aside his personal wishes in favor of what he thought was the public good? Have you ever had to set aside your personal beliefs or wishes for the greater good of the group? If so, explain.

If not, could you imagine making such a sacrifice? Explain why or why not.

★ Fort Sumter ★

The Civil War officially began when the South Carolina militia attacked Fort Sumter, the federal garrison in the harbor at Charleston, South Carolina, on April 12, 1861. It was surrendered the next day. Two days after that, President Abraham Lincoln (1809–1865) declared a state of

"insurrection," and called for 75,000 volunteers for three months' service.

Imagine you are living in the Union but have a relative who lives in the Confederacy. Write a letter to your relative telling how you feel about the war and the prospect of fighting against each other in battle.

★ The Emancipation ★ Proclamation

In 1863, President Abraham Lincoln (1809–1865) signed the Emancipation Proclamation, freeing all slaves in the rebelling states. Before that time, Lincoln said his goal was to preserve the Union, slave or free.

How do you think the passage of the Emancipation Proclamation would have changed the war and how people—northerners and southerners, slaveholders and non slaveholders—felt about the Civil War?

★ The Draft ★

The Conscription Act of 1863 required all men between 20 and 45 years of age to sign up for military service. Service could be avoided by paying $300 to the federal government or by hiring a substitute to serve in your place.

Do you think the Conscription Act of 1863 was fair in its provisions that allowed men to pay for release from service or hire a substitute? How do you think rich people felt about these provisions? How do you think poor people felt? Would you ever pay for someone to go to war for you? Would you ever take money to go to war in someone's place? Give reasons for your answers.

★ The Gettysburg Address ★

On November 19, 1863, President Abraham Lincoln (1809–1865) dedicated a military cemetery on the battlefield at Gettysburg, Pennsylvania. The speech that Lincoln gave that day was one of the greatest ever made:

"Fourscore and seven years ago our fathers brought forth on this continent a new nation, conceived in liberty and dedicated to the proposition that all men are created equal. Now we are engaged in a great civil war, testing whether that nation or any nation so conceived and so dedicated can long endure. We are met on a great battlefield of that war. We have come to dedicate a portion of that field as a final resting-place for those who here gave their lives that that nation might live. It is altogether fitting and proper that we should do this. But in a larger sense, we cannot dedicate, we cannot consecrate, we cannot hallow this ground. The brave men, living and dead, who struggled here have consecrated it far above our poor power to add or detract. The world will little note nor long remember what we say here, but it can never forget what they did here. It is for us the living rather to be dedicated here to the unfinished work which they who fought here have thus far so nobly advanced. It is rather for us to be here dedicated to the great task remaining before us—that from these honored dead we take increased devotion to that cause for which they gave the last full measure of devotion—that we here highly resolve that these dead shall not have died in vain, that this nation under God shall have a new birth of freedom, and that government of the people, by the people, for the people shall not perish from the earth."

How does this speech make you feel? Tell whether or not you think it's a good speech, and why. What do you think makes a good speech?

★ Sherman's March to the Sea ★

In May 1864, General William Tecumseh Sherman (1820–1891) invaded Georgia with 100,000 Union troops. By September, Sherman had taken Atlanta. The general then marched his troops to the Atlantic Coast, destroying everything in his path. Sherman's tactics are now known as a "total war," meaning not just a war against an enemy army, but a war against enemy civilians, as well.

What do you think of the tactic of "total war"? Do you agree with the old saying, "All is fair in love and war"? Explain your thinking.

★ Lee Surrenders at ★ Appomattox

On the morning of April 9, 1865, Confederate General Robert E. Lee (1807–1870) surrendered to Union General Ulysses S. Grant (1822–1885). Grant later recalled the surrender in his memoirs: "What General Lee's feelings were I do not know . . . but my own feelings . . . were sad and depressed. I felt like anything rather than rejoicing at the downfall of a foe who

had fought so long and valiantly and had suffered so much . . . ."

Have you, like Grant, ever won something and had mixed feelings about your victory? What was your experience? How did you feel? Why do you think you felt that way?

★ Lincoln's Assassination ★

John Wilkes Booth (1838–1865), a fanatical supporter of the South, assassinated President Abraham Lincoln (1809–1865) while Lincoln watched a play at Ford's Theater on April 14, 1865. American poet Walt Whitman (1819–1892) went on to write the poem, "O Captain! My Captain!"

O Captain! my Captain! our fearful trip is
    done,
The ship has weather'd every rack, the
    prize we sought is won,
The port is near, the bells I hear, the people
    all exulting,
While follow eyes the steady keel, the vessel
    grim and daring;
But O heart! heart! heart!
O the bleeding drops of red,
    Where on the deck my Captain lies,
        Fallen cold and dead.

Who is the Captain that Whitman writes of in this poem? What is the ship? What is the prize? Based on this poem, do you think Whitman supported the Union or the Confederacy? Compose your own short poem about the Civil War and Lincoln's death.

★ Reconstruction ★

The South was devastated—physically, economically, and spiritually—after the Civil War. Lincoln's plan had been to bring the rebellious states back into the Union with as little trouble for them as possible. After Lincoln's death, his successor Andrew Johnson (1808–1875), wanted to follow Lincoln's plan, but Radical Republicans wanted to make it much more difficult for the states that had seceded to rejoin the Union. The Radical Republicans were more powerful than Johnson, and had their way. They divided the South into military regions under the command of generals. They also required the states to adopt constitutions that allowed blacks to vote and to accept the Fourteenth Amendment, which extended citizenship to blacks.

Write a paragraph in favor of moderate reconstruction and one in favor of harsher reconstruction. Which argument do you think is stronger? Defend your reasoning. Why do you think many northerners wanted to make readmission to the Union difficult for the rebellious states?

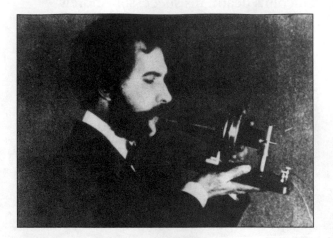

★ Telephone! ★

Alexander Graham Bell (1847–1922) made the world's first phone call in 1876. His invention quickly caught on and has become one of the most important utilities today.

How important is the telephone to you? What are some of the ways in which you use it? How would your life be different if the telephone had never been invented?

★ The Wizard of Menlo Park ★

Thomas Alva Edison (1847–1931) became known as the "Wizard of Menlo Park" because of the many inventions that came out of his laboratory in Menlo Park, New Jersey. The most famous of these was the incandescent lamp, but the laboratory had more than 1,000 patents for inventions created by Edison and his staff.

Imagine you're applying for a job at Thomas Edison's laboratory. Write a description of an invention you would like to make to show you're the right person for the job.

★ Lights Out? ★

After Thomas Edison (1847–1931) died on October 18, 1931, there were plans to dim the lights of the entire country for a full minute as a memorial tribute to their inventor. But in the end, the plans had to be scrapped—electric light had become too important to do without.

What do you think could have happened if the lights went out for a full minute across the nation? Brainstorm a list of possible occurrences. Then write an imaginary news story about what happened in one town—maybe yours—during the one-minute memorial.

★ The Wright Brothers ★

Orville (1871–1948) and Wilbur Wright (1867–1912) made the world's first successful flights in a motorized aircraft near Kitty Hawk, North Carolina, in 1903.

Imagine you could fly like a bird. What do you think it would be like?

★ The Ford Model T ★

Henry Ford (1864–1947) did not invent the automobile, but he did help bring the fairly new German invention to the masses. He did this by designing a simple, sturdy automobile called the Model T, and developing assembly-line techniques to build it. The result was an affordable car and a change in the way Americans lived.

In what ways do you think the Ford Model T changed America? Think of the way people lived and worked as well as the landscape of the country.

★ Mass Production ★

In 1908, Henry Ford (1864–1947) manufactured 10,607 cars that sold for $850 each. In 1916, he produced 730,041 cars that sold for $360 each. Ford was able to produce more cars and sell them for less money by perfecting his assembly-line techniques.

How do assembly lines affect the consumer? How do they affect the worker? Do you think assembly lines are good or bad things? Explain.

★ Inventions ★

The telephone, the lightbulb, the automobile, and the airplane are among the many great inventions made after the Civil War.

Which invention—the telephone, the light bulb, the automobile, or the airplane—do you think is the most important, and why?

Big Business, Labor, and Government

★ Robber Barons ★

In the late 1800s, many men made fortunes by taking unfair advantage of natural resources, cheap labor, or their influence over the government to build up their businesses. These men became known as robber barons.

What do you think would drive a person to become a so-called robber baron? Do you think the way such people run their businesses is wrong? Explain whether or not you think there are robber barons today.

★ Monopoly ★

A monopoly is a company or group of companies that controls the supply of a product or a service. In the late 1800s, individuals such as John D. Rockefeller (1839–1937) and J. P. Morgan (1837–1913) established large monopolies that came to be known as trusts.

Imagine there is only one company that makes blue jeans. How do you think that would affect the price, supply, and variety of blue jeans available? Do you think that any monopolies exist today? If so, what, if anything, should be done about them?

★ Andrew Carnegie's "Gospel of Wealth" ★

Andrew Carnegie (1835–1919) made a fortune in the steel industry and went on to give a good deal of it away. In an 1889 speech, "The Gospel of Wealth," Carnegie proclaimed that the rich had a responsibility to use their money to help others. He said, "The man who dies . . . rich dies disgraced."

Do you agree with Carnegie that the rich have an obligation to help others? Explain your reasons. If you had millions of dollars, what would you do with it? Would you feel you should help others less fortunate than you? Give reasons for your answer.

★ Labor Unions ★

In the late 19th century, most working people suffered long hours, low pay, and hazardous conditions at the hands of their employers. Despite these conditions, many refused to join labor unions that

had been organized to fight for better treatment of workers. They feared they would lose their jobs, as employers often found some reason to fire such "trouble-makers."

Imagine you're working in a cotton mill or a coal mine in the late 19th century. Your family needs your income to help put food on the table and keep the roof over your heads, but you work long hours in dangerous conditions. You work 14 hours a day, six days a week, and have seen co-workers lose lives and limbs on the job. What would you do if someone asked you to join a labor union to fight for better working conditions? Would you join, even if it meant you might lose your job? Or would you refuse to join, and accept your employer's unreasonable demands?

★ Dangerous Working ★ Conditions

On January 10, 1860, there was a terrible accident at Pemberton Mill in Lawrence, Massachusetts. Seventy-seven people—mostly girls less than 12 years old—died when the building collapsed on them. The victims' families were given very little compensation. One observer called it "the respectable millionaire homicide."

Do you think rich people are held to a different set of laws than other people? Explain.

★ Haymarket Square Strike ★

On May 3, 1886, police fired into a crowd of striking workers at McCormick Reaper Company in Chicago, killing four people. The strikers held a protest rally the next day at Haymarket Square. A bomb exploded during the rally and killed seven police officers. The rally's organizers were quickly arrested and convicted, despite the fact that the actual bomber was never identified. Four men were hanged and three were jailed. Illinois governor John Peter Altgeld (1847–1902) pardoned the three survivors in 1893, a move that ruined his political career.

Do you think the organizers of the rally should have been convicted? What do you think of Governor Altgeld? Would you have done as he did and pardoned the survivors? Would you have done so even if you knew it would cost you your career? Have you ever had to make a decision where doing what was right would hurt you in some way? Explain.

★ Child Labor ★

Mary Harris Jones, also called Mother Jones, was a well-known union organizer at the turn of the century. In 1903, she led a "March of the Mill Children" from Philadelphia to New York City. The young workers carried placards that read, "We want to go to school," and "We want time to play." As a result of the march,

Pennsylvania made child labor illegal.

Why do you think children were sent to work in the first place? How do you think children and families felt when child labor laws were passed? Why might these laws have been viewed as a mixed blessing? What do you think could have been done to make child labor unnecessary?

★ Jane Addams and Hull House ★

Jane Addams (1860–1935) was a wealthy, well educated young woman who wanted to improve the lives of the poor. In 1889, she opened the doors to Hull House in Chicago's poverty-ridden West Side. The house became the most famous settlement house—a house in a slum where university-trained people would settle to help relieve poverty—in the country.

If you were wealthy and well educated, would you want to "share the lives of the poor," as Jane Addams did? Do you think the only way you could help the poor is by going to live with them? How else could you help the poor?

★ Political Corruption ★

Business wasn't the only way to get rich in the late 19th century—there was also politics. The Tweed Ring, a group of corrupt New York City officials led by William March Tweed (1823–1878), is believed to have stolen anywhere from $40 million to $200 million in public funds. Many of these men saw no wrong in what they did. One of Tweed's cohorts, George Washington Plunkett, explained his form of "honest graft" to a journalist as follows: "I seen my opportunities and I took 'em . . . I'm tipped off, say, that they are going to lay out a new park at a certain place . . . . I go to that place and I buy up all the land I can and then there is a rush to get my land. Ain't it perfectly honest to charge a good price and make a profit on my investment and foresight? Of course, it is. Well, that's honest graft."

Do you agree that there is such a thing as "honest graft"? Do you think politicians should be allowed to profit from insider information?

★ "Speak Softly, and Carry ★ a Big Stick"

A favorite saying of President Theodore Roosevelt's (1858–1919) was an old African proverb, "Speak softly, and carry a big stick; you will go far."

What do you think this African proverb means? Tell whether or not it's a philosophy you would like to adopt in your life.

How might a president use that philosophy to settle a dispute with a neighboring country?

★ The Panama Canal ★

In 1903, a ship had to sail around the tip of South America to get from the Atlantic Ocean to the Pacific Ocean, a journey that took about two months. Many people, including President Theodore Roosevelt (1858–1919), wanted a quicker route, and building a canal across the Isthmus of Panama looked like the way to go. But Colombia refused to sign a treaty that would allow the United States to build a canal across its territory in Panama. Roosevelt did not let Colombia get in the way of his dream, however. He quickly supported a revolution to make Panama an independent country, one that was happy to let the United States build a canal through it.

Do you think Roosevelt was right in helping to create a new country in order to get his canal built? Do you agree with the saying, "The end justifies the means"? Explain why or why not.

★ Theodore Roosevelt and ★ Conservation

President Theodore Roosevelt (1858–1919) loved the outdoors and often talked about the importance of conservation, of protecting our land and natural resources. President Roosevelt once said, "The rights

of the public to natural resources outweigh private rights, and must be given first consideration."

Do you agree with Roosevelt's belief that public rights outweigh private rights in the area of conservation? Who do you think would support this belief? Who do you think would oppose it?

★ Progressivism and ★ Muckrakers

The widespread greed and corruption that followed the Civil War led to a reform movement called Progressivism. Progressive writers wrote about corrupt governments, crime- and disease-ridden slums, and horrendous working conditions, among other things. These writers were known as muckrakers, after a character in a 17th-century book (John Bunyan's *Pilgrim's Progress*) who used a "muckrake" to clean up the moral filth around him.

Do you think writers can help improve the way people live? Tell how. What do you think you could change by writing about it?

★ Yellow Journalism ★

Yellow journalism is the practice of publishing stories to increase newspaper sales, regardless of whether the stories are true. It got its name from the publication of "The Yellow Kid of Hogan's Alley," a comic published by the *New York World* in 1905. The comic used a new color process to make its main character yellow. The comic was a hit and helped the *World* close the gap with its rival, *The New York Journal*. Then the *Journal's* publisher, William Randolph Hearst (1863–1951), lured the "Yellow Kid" cartoonist from the *World's* publisher, Joseph Pulitzer (1847–1911). The newspaper giants continued to try to outdo each other, often with sensational news stories that stretched the truth in order to attract readers.

Write a short news article about something that happened to you. Then rewrite the article using "yellow journalism"— twisting the facts to make it even more appealing to readers.

★ The Spanish-American War ★

The Spanish-American War (1898) was fought between the United States and Spain for Cuba's independence. At the time, Cuba and Puerto Rico were the only two Spanish colonies left in North America.

Do you think the United States has a right to interfere in the affairs of other countries? Give reasons to support your answer.

★ "Feeding Prisoners to Sharks" ★

Newspapers fighting for readers helped bring about the Spanish-American War (1898) with sensational headlines like, "Feeding Prisoners to Sharks." The newspapers were aware of their power. *New York Journal* publisher William Randolph Hearst (1863–1951) hired the painter Frederic Remington (1861–1909) to go to Cuba and paint what was happening there. When Remington cabled Hearst, "Everything quiet. There is no trouble. There will be no war. I wish to return," Hearst cabled back, "Please remain. You furnish the pictures and I'll furnish the war."

How could newspapers help start a war? Think about how facts can be twisted, then try your own biased reporting. Make a list of facts about candy. Write one paragraph that uses some or all of these facts to tell why eating candy is bad for you, and another that uses the same facts to tell why eating candy is good for you.

Immigration

★ Ellis Island ★

Ellis Island was opened on January 1, 1892. The immigration center helped send many newcomers to the United States on their way, but sent back those who were sick or otherwise deemed unfit to live in this country.

Where did your ancestors come from? 3/24 *How might your life be different if your ancestors had been sent back to their native countries?*

★ "Give Me Your Tired, ★ Your Poor . . ."

Millions of immigrants who passed through Ellis Island were welcomed by the sight of the Statue of Liberty on Bledsoe Island in New York Harbor. The base of the statue is inscribed with a poem written by American poet Emma Lazarus (1849–1887):

". . . Give me your tired, your poor,
　Your huddled masses yearning to
　breathe free,
The wretched refuse of your teeming shore.
Send these, the homeless, tempest-tossed
　to me,
I lift my lamp beside the golden door!"

Imagine you are an immigrant seeking freedom from war in Russia or hunger in Ireland. Write how you would feel seeing the Statue of Liberty after your long voyage across the Atlantic.

★ Immigration Restrictions ★

Throughout history, Congress has passed laws to restrict immigration. Sometimes these laws were aimed at specific countries, like the 1882 Chinese Exclusion Act, which barred Chinese laborers from entering the United States for 10 years. Others were aimed at entire regions, such as the Johnson-Reed Immigration Act of 1924, which limited immigration from Europe. Others were aimed at classes of people, such as an 1882 immigration act that barred entry to criminals, paupers, and the insane, among others.

Why do you think Congress passed some

of these restriction acts? Do you think Congress always acted honorably? Should anyone who wants to live in the United States be able to live here, or should there be some restrictions on immigration? Defend your thinking. If you believe there should be restrictions, explain what they should be.

★ The First Immigrants ★

The first immigrants came to this land anywhere from 10,000 to 45,000 years ago, crossed a land bridge that once existed across the Bering Sea to migrate from northeast Asia to northwest North America. These immigrants were the ancestors of Native Americans.

Think of all the immigrants that came to this land after the Native Americans. What do you think a Native American might have to say about current efforts to limit immigration?

★ A Different Perspective ★

Until this century, most of America's history has been recorded and written by white men.

How is it determined who records a country's history? Do you think written history can be biased? Defend your view. How might our American history be different if told from the perspective of, say, black women? Some time in the 21st century, people of Hispanic heritage will become the largest single ethnic group in the United States. Do you think our history will be rewritten when our country has an Hispanic majority? Do you think it should be? Explain why or why not.

World War I and The Great Depression

★ Minding Our Own Business ★

When World War I erupted in Europe in the summer of 1914, most Americans wanted no part in the war. Neutralism—a policy to not get involved with either side in a dispute—was an important part of United States foreign policy at the time. We took care of business in our own hemisphere, period. The United States' eventual entry into the war forever changed our foreign policy. We were no longer a country that minded its own business; we were a world power that looked out for the rest of the world.

What do you think of the policy of neutralism? Should the United States should go back to that policy? Tell why or why not. How do you feel about the policy of neutralism in your personal life? When should you mind your own business? When should you get involved in other people's disputes?

★ Wilson's War Request ★

In his War Request to Congress on April 2, 1917, President Woodrow Wilson (1856–1924) said, "It is a fearful thing to lead this great peaceful people into war, into the most terrible and disastrous of all wars, civilization itself seeming to be in the balance. But the right is more precious than peace, and we shall fight for the things which we have carried nearest our hearts—for democracy. . . ."

Do you think world democracy is worth fighting for? What things, if any, would you risk your life fighting for?

★ Support or Silence ★

Although many Americans supported the United States' involvement in World War I, there were some who objected to spilling our young men's blood in a "foreign war." President Woodrow Wilson (1856–1924) did everything in his power to encourage support for the war and silence its critics. To drum up support, he had films, posters,

and pamphlets produced to show the "Great War," as it was called, as a clear contest between good and evil. Critics who refused to believe in this black-and-white scenario were silenced and censored with the use of emergency war powers.

Why do you think President Wilson used the government's powers to increase support of the war and to silence critics? Was he was right to do this? Are such methods used today? Do you think these methods are helpful or harmful to Americans—to both those at home and those fighting?

★ War: Good for Business ★

Before President Woodrow Wilson (1856–1924) made his War Request to Congress, a member of the New York Stock Exchange wrote a letter in favor of the United States entering the war, saying it would be good for business.

How could being at war be good for business? Do you think a war's effect on business should ever be taken into consideration when deciding whether or not to enter a war? Do you believe it ever is taken into consideration? Who might benefit from the business of war? Who might lose? Is this fair?

★ Black Tuesday ★

The 1920s were prosperous for most Americans. One need only look at the price of stocks (shares of ownership in compa-

nies). For most of the 1920s, stock prices went up. Many people bought stocks on credit, because they were sure stock prices could only keep rising. In the fall of 1929, they were proven wrong. Stock prices started to fall. Many people panicked and began trying to sell their stocks. With so many sellers and very few buyers, stock prices fell even further. Then, on October 29, stock prices plummeted. People lost fortunes. Many who had bought stock on credit found themselves deeply in debt. The day became known as "Black Tuesday."

Think about how the people who bought stocks on credit were hurt by the stock market crash. What do you think of credit? Do you think people should borrow money to buy things? Have you ever borrowed money for something and later wished you hadn't?

★ Hoovervilles ★

When the stock market crashed in 1929, most Americans believed in a very limited role for the federal government. They felt that the government should not be in the business of helping people and that people should take care of themselves. That was the belief of then-President Herbert Hoover (1874–1964). But there were many people who needed help. Among them were the thousands left homeless after the stock market crash. They were forced to live in boxes and crates in shantytowns that became known as "Hoovervilles," for the president who refused to help them.

How much responsibility, if any, do you think the American government should have for the well-being of its citizens? What are some ways the American government helps take care of its citizens today? Do you believe the government is right in taking these responsibilities?

★ Keeping Up Appearances ★

President Herbert Hoover (1874–1964) believed keeping up appearances was good for national morale. So, despite the rampant hunger and homelessness of the Great Depression, he and the First Lady continued to be called to dinner by buglers and to eat seven-course meals served by a small army of white-gloved servants.

Do you agree or disagree with President Hoover that it is important for a leader to keep up appearances? How do you think President Hoover should have lived during the Great Depression? If you had been president then, how would you have lived?

★ Franklin Delano Roosevelt ★

When Franklin Delano Roosevelt (1882–1945) was 41 years old, he was crippled by polio. His mother urged him to retire, but his wife persuaded him to return to public life. With hard work and determination, FDR learned to stand using iron leg braces and to walk with the aid of crutches. He ran for governor of New York and won. When Roosevelt decided to run for president, his opponents said his physical condition, among other things, made him unfit for the White House.

Do you think that a person's physical limitations have anything to do with how well he or she can govern? What qualities do you think make a person fit to be president?

★ Overcoming Obstacles ★

Franklin Delano Roosevelt (1882–1945) would later recall how his 1921 bout with polio and its crippling effects taught him to be a fighter: "Once I spent two years lying in bed, trying to move my big toe. That was the hardest job I ever had to do. After that, anything seems easy."

How can overcoming obstacles help make a person stronger? What difficulties have you or someone you know had to face in life? How has dealing with them made you or that person stronger?

★ "The Only Thing We ★ Have to Fear . . ."

In his first inaugural address, on March 4, 1933, President Franklin Delano Roosevelt (1882–1945) promised a brighter future to the nation. He said, "Let me assert my firm belief that the only thing we have to fear is fear itself."

What did President Roosevelt mean by this remark? Describe a time when fear held you back. How can fear be helpful? How can it be harmful?

★ The New Deal ★

President Franklin Delano Roosevelt (1882–1945) had promised the American people a New Deal to lift the country out of depression. One of the most controversial parts of the New Deal was the National Recovery Act (NRA), which, among other things, set minimum wages and maximum working hours. The business community fought FDR on the NRA but lost.

Why do you suppose the business community fought the National Recovery Act? Who do you think supported it? Should the federal government set minimum wages and maximum working hours?

World War II

★ "Four Essential Freedoms" ★

In his address to Congress on January 6, 1941, President Franklin Delano Roosevelt (1882–1945) said:

"In the future days, which we seek to make secure, we look forward to a world founded upon four essential freedoms.

The first is freedom of speech and expression—everywhere in the world.

The second is freedom of every person to worship God in his own way—everywhere in the world.

The third is freedom from want . . .

The fourth is freedom from fear."

Which of these freedoms do you think is most important, and why?

★ Pearl Harbor ★

On the morning of December 7, 1941, Japan launched an air attack on Pearl Harbor, Hawaii. The attack took 2,403 American lives, sunk or seriously damaged 18 U.S. Navy ships, and destroyed nearly 200 U.S. airplanes. In his war message to Congress the following day, President Franklin Delano Roosevelt (1882–1945) called December 7, 1941, "a date which will live in infamy."

Write a newspaper editorial arguing why the Japanese attack on Pearl Harbor should or should not lead the United States into World War II.

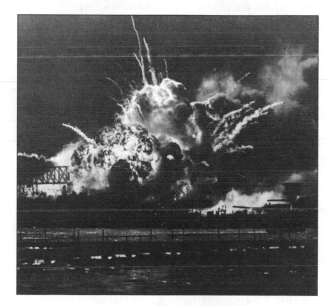

★ Japanese-American ★ Internment Camps

After Japan's attack on Pearl Harbor, many Californians began to fear that Japanese-Americans were spying for Japan. President Franklin Delano Roosevelt (1882–1945) responded to pressures from West Coast politicians to do something about these fears by signing Executive Order 9066 on February 19, 1942. This law required all

Japanese Americans living within 200 miles of the Pacific coast to move out of their homes and into internment camps in Colorado, Utah, Arkansas, and other interior states. More than 100,000 Japanese Americans, citizens and noncitizens, lost their homes and possessions in this relocation.

Do you think it was right to remove Japanese Americans from their homes and send them to internment camps after the Japanese attacked Pearl Harbor? Imagine you were a Japanese-American citizen in 1941 and 1942. How would you have felt when Japan bombed Pearl Harbor? How would you have felt when you received an order to move?

★ The Holocaust ★

When the Allies were closing in on Berlin in the spring of 1945, they entered Hitler's concentration camps. The Nazis sent Jews, Gypsies, Slavs, homosexuals, and others believed "undesirable" to these camps to be killed in gas chambers. The Nazis murdered 12 million people in these death camps, about 6 million of them Jews. This murder of Jews because of prejudice and hate by the Nazis is called the Holocaust.

What can be done about prejudice and hate so that history never again sees something as horrible as the Holocaust?

★ How Did Concentration ★ Camps Happen?

After World War II, many people wondered how such a horrific thing as the concentration camps could ever have been allowed to happen. German minister Martin Niemoeller gave this answer:

"In Germany, they first came for the Communists, and I didn't speak up because I wasn't a Communist. Then they came for the Jews, and I didn't speak up because I wasn't a Jew. Then they came for the trade unionists, and I didn't speak up because I wasn't a trade unionist. Then they came for the Catholics, and I didn't speak up because I was a Protestant. Then they came for me, and by that time no one was left to speak up."

What does this quote say about how concentration camps came to be? What does it tell us about seeing that they never happen again?

★ Truman's Choice— ★ The Atomic Bomb

After their victory in Europe, the Allies focused their attention on the war with Japan. President Harry S. Truman (1884–1972) was faced with an awful decision. He could invade Japan, a move that would cost the Allies an estimated one million lives, or he could use a terrible new weapon, the nuclear bomb, against Japan. President Truman chose the bomb. On August 6, 1945, a U.S. B-29 bomber dropped the

most destructive weapon the world had ever known on Hiroshima, Japan. In less than a second, more than half of the city's 300,000 population was killed, wounded, or missing. Three days later, Truman ordered another bomb dropped on Nagasaki, Japan. The results were almost equally devastating. Japan surrendered on August 14. World War II was over.

What would you have done if you were in President Truman's shoes—would you have authorized an invasion of Japan and risked a million Allied lives, or would you have authorized the use of the atomic bomb? Explain your decision.

The Cold War

★ Iron Curtain ★

On March 5, 1946, British Prime Minister Winston Churchill (1874–1965) spoke of the economic, social, and military barriers created against the West by the Soviet Union and Eastern European communist countries. "From Stettin in the Baltic to Trieste in the Adriatic," he said, "an iron curtain has descended across the continent."

What does the expression "Iron Curtain" make you think of? Is it positive or negative, and why?

★ The Arms Race ★

In the cold war between the United States and the Soviet Union, each side began building bigger and more powerful weapons. By the 1950s, both sides had built hydrogen bombs—nuclear weapons that were even more powerful than the atomic bombs dropped on Hiroshima and Nagasaki. President Dwight D. Eisenhower (1890–1969), thinking of possible nuclear warfare, said, "War has become not just tragic, but preposterous. With modern weapons, there can be no victory for anyone."

What did President Eisenhower mean by this remark? Do you agree or disagree

with him? Why? What do you think can be done to avoid the possibility of such a "preposterous" war?

★ McCarthyism ★

Senator Joseph R. McCarthy (1908–1957) made a name for himself in the early 1950s when he fought to get communists out of the government and other positions of power. It wasn't a very clean fight, though. McCarthy pointed fingers and made groundless accusations that, with the support of the media and the American people, stuck. The careers and reputations of the accused were ruined. President Eisenhower (1890–1969) finally put a stop to the smear campaign when McCarthy accused the U.S. Army of being full of communists.

Why is it important not to believe everything we hear in the news? What might happen if we believed everything we heard?

★ Blacklisted! ★

One of the groups that Senator McCarthy (1908-1957) believed was riddled with communists (see above) was the

Hollywood film industry. During his investigations, the accused were asked to reveal the names of communists. Those who refused to incriminate others were blacklisted, or put on a list of persons whom no studio would hire.

Imagine you're a Hollywood filmmaker in the 1950's whom Senator McCarthy has accused of being a communist. If you had to choose between naming names and incriminating others or being blacklisted, what would you do? Defend your actions.

★ *"Ich Bin Ein Berliner"* ★

When President John F. Kennedy (1917–1963) visited a divided Germany in 1963, he spoke these words at City Hall in the capital of West Berlin: "All free men, wherever they may live, are citizens of Berlin. And therefore, as a free man, I take pride in the words *Ich bin ein Berliner.*"

What do you think President Kennedy meant when he spoke the words, "I am a Berliner"? Do you feel at one with people in other parts of the world? What do such feelings mean for world peace?

★ **Tearing Down the Berlin Wall** ★

The opening of the Berlin Wall in November 1989 symbolized the end of the Cold War. This 110-mile-long wall had been built by Communist East Germany in 1961 to keep its citizens from fleeing to the West. Up until then, large numbers of East Germans had fled to the West. Many people still tried to escape, and some made it, but more than 170 others lost their lives in the attempt. In 1989, popular protests against travel and emigration restrictions forced the East German government to open the wall. By the end of the next year, East Germany and West Germany had joined to become the non-Communist country of Germany.

What does it say about a country if the government has to build walls to keep its people from leaving? What are some ways to keep people from leaving a country without building a wall? Think about why the United States doesn't need a wall to keep its citizens from leaving.

Civil Rights

★ Invisible Man ★

In his 1952 book *Invisible Man*, Ralph Ellison (1914–1994) described what it was like to be a black man: "I am invisible, understand, simply because people refuse to see me."

Have you ever felt invisible? If so, how did it make you feel? If not, how do you imagine it would feel? What might you do to try to make yourself visible?

★ Separate but Equal? ★

The Supreme Court declared segregation constitutional in the landmark 1896 case *Plessy v. Ferguson*. In his majority opinion, Justice Henry Brown wrote that he could not agree "that the enforced separation of the two races stamps the colored race with a badge of inferiority. If this be so, it is not the reason of anything found in the act, but solely because the colored race chooses to put that construction upon it." The Supreme Court declared segregation illegal 68 years later in its 1954 ruling on *Brown v. Board of Education* of Topeka. Chief Justice Earl Warren (1891–1974) wrote,

"We conclude that in the field of public education the doctrine of 'separate but equal' has no place. Separate educational facilities are inherently unequal . . . . To separate them [children] from others of similar age and qualifications solely because of their race generates a feeling of inferiority as to their status in the community that may affect their hearts and minds in a way unlikely ever to be undone . . . ."

Imagine Justice Henry Brown and Justice Earl Warren are contemporaries. Choose one of their opinions and write an argument trying to convince the other justice of its truth.

★ Little Rock, Arkansas ★

In September 1957, Arkansas governor Orville Faubus used 270 armed men from the Arkansas National Guard to prevent nine black children from entering the previously all-white Little Rock Central High School. A federal court order forced Faubus to withdraw the national guard, which he did, but the students were then left to the mercy of angry mobs trying to block their entrance. Finally, President Dwight D. Eisenhower (1890–1969) had to send 1,100 paratroopers to Little Rock and place the Arkansas National Guard under his direct orders so the children could enter

the school. The troops had to stay for the entire school year to protect the students from nearly constant harassment. Despite the difficulties they faced, eight of the children finished the school year.

Why do you think the nine black students who tried to enter Little Rock Central High School in 1957 were willing to face such obstacles to go to that school? Would you be willing to face the same type of experience? What do you think the students needed to survive the year at the school?

★ Rosa Parks ★

On December 1, 1955, Rosa Parks boarded a city bus in Montgomery, Alabama, on her way home from work. There were no seats in the "negro section" in the back of the bus, so she took a seat in the middle of the bus. When the bus became crowded and whites had nowhere to sit, the bus driver asked Parks to give her seat to a white person. She refused and was jailed.

Imagine you were on the bus with Rosa Parks. Write a letter to a friend telling about the event and what, if anything, you think it bodes for the future. You can write from the viewpoint of a white person or a black person.

★ Montgomery Bus Boycott ★

For a year after Rosa Parks's arrest, African Americans refused to ride buses in Montgomery, Alabama. This boycott meant that many black people had to walk long distances to and from work and school. Martin Luther King, Jr. (1929– 1968), one of the boycott's leaders, asked an elderly woman if her feet were tired from so much walking. She replied, "Yes, my feet are tired, but my soul is rested."

What do you think the woman meant by her response?

★ "I Have a Dream" ★

On August 28, 1963, Martin Luther King, Jr. (1929–1968), spoke these words from the steps of the Lincoln Memorial in Washington, D.C., to a quarter of a million people:

"I say to you today, my friends, that in spite of the difficulties and frustrations of the moment I still have a dream. It is a dream deeply rooted in the American dream.

I have a dream that one day this nation will rise up and live out the true meaning of its creed: 'We hold these truths to be self-evi-

dent; that all men are created equal.'

I have a dream that one day on the red hills of Georgia the sons of former slaves and the sons of former slaveowners will be able to sit down together at the table of brotherhood . . . .

I have a dream that my four children will one day live in a nation where they will not be judged by the color of their skin but by the content of their character.

I have a dream today . . . ."

Do you believe Martin Luther King's dream has come true? Write your own "I Have a Dream" speech, telling what you would like to see in America's future.

★ Civil Disobedience Versus ★ Aggression

By the early 1960s, the civil rights movement was showing a split. On the one hand were the supporters of Martin Luther King, Jr. (1929–1968), who believed that civil disobedience, such as the Montgomery bus boycott, was the road to a better future. On the other hand were the supporters of Malcolm X (1925–1965),

who believed that they could only reach their goals through aggression and violence.

Compare civil disobedience and violence as ways of achieving a goal. Which do you think is more effective, and why? Is there is a proper time for each? Explain your thinking.

★ Economic Equality ★

Martin Luther King, Jr. (1929–1968), once said, "I worked to get these people the right to eat hamburgers, and now I've got to do something to help them get the money to buy them."

What do you think King meant by this? How important is economic equality to overall equality?

★ Civil Rights Act of 1964 ★

The Civil Rights Act of 1964 made segregation and discrimination in such public places as restaurants, theaters, and hotels illegal. It also made it against the law for employers to hire workers based on race.

Do you believe that once something is made law, it becomes so? What besides laws do you think is needed to change the way people live and act?

Women's Rights

★ "Remember the Ladies" ★

At the time of the American Revolution, women had few rights. They could not vote or hold public office. They could not attend college. And, once married, their husbands had almost complete legal control over them. Abigail Adams (1744–1818) hoped that the nation's independence might mean more freedom for women. She wrote the following in a letter to her husband, John, when he was in the Continental Congress, "In the new code of laws which I suppose it will be necessary for you to make, I desire that you would remember the ladies . . . . Do not put such unlimited power in the hands of husbands." John Adams wrote back, "As to your extraordinary code of laws, I cannot but laugh."

Imagine you are Abigail Adams and have just received John's response to your request that he "remember the ladies." Write a letter back to him explaining how you feel.

★ Free Blacks, but not Women ★

Most male abolitionists fought hard to free black people, but did not support equal rights for women. In fact, it was a slight on the part of such male abolitionists—they told Elizabeth Cady Stanton (1815–1902) and Lucretia Mott (1793–1880) to sit in the balcony at an antislavery meeting—that led these two women to call for a women's convention at Seneca Falls, New York.

Do you see anything ironic in male abolitionists fighting to end slavery but refusing to treat women as their equals? Explain your answer.

★ Seneca Falls ★

The women's movement in America started at a women's convention at Seneca Falls, New York, on July 19, 1848. The convention, organized by Elizabeth Cady Stanton (1815–1902) and Lucretia Mott (1793–1880), approved a "Declaration of Sentiments on the Rights of Women." The beginning of the declaration said that "all men and women are created equal." It went on to ask for women to have the right to vote, the right to own property, the right to keep earned wages, and the right to a college education.

Think about the rights asked for at the 1848 Seneca Falls women's rights

convention. Which right do you feel is the most important, and why?

★ Sojourner Truth ★

Former slave Sojourner Truth (1797–1883) spoke at a second women's rights convention in 1851. In response to men's arguments that women were weak and needed protection and not equal rights, she answered: "Look at me! Look at my arm! I have plowed and planted . . . . And ain't I a woman? I could work as much and eat as much as a man . . . and bear the lash as well—and ain't I a woman?"

Imagine you're one of the men arguing that women need protection, not equal rights. Do Sojourner Truth's words move you in any way, or cause you to think differently? Explain why or why not.

★ Flowers or Vegetables? ★ Pretty or Useful?

Henry T. Finck wrote the following in the April 1901 issue of *The Independent*: "One of the most important problems to be solved in the new century is this: Shall women be flowers or vegetables? Pretty or useful? In other words, shall women work?"

Write a short essay about what problems facing women should be solved in the 21st century.

★ Picket Power ★

Democratic President Woodrow Wilson (1856–1924) opposed the vote for women. In 1916, suffragist Alice Paul (1885–1977) and others protested by picketing around the clock outside the White House. The protesters were arrested, but not before getting attention and sympathy for their cause. They got more of both when they went on hunger strikes before finally being released from jail. These tactics helped elect a Republican Congress in 1918 that included Jeannette Rankin (1880–1973) from Montana, the first woman elected to Congress. Rankin's first act was to introduce a constitutional suffrage amendment onto the House floor. The Nineteenth Amendment, which gives women the right to vote, was ratified on August 26, 1920.

Think of a law you would like changed. How would you go about trying to get it changed? Do you agree or disagree with the methods Alice Paul and others used to help win women the right to vote? Explain your thinking.

★ Rosie the Riveter ★

Rosie the Riveter was the symbol of American women during World War II. Before then, most women worked in the home. But the United States needed military and industrial strength to fight the war. The men provided the military strength, but that left the factories without workers. During the war, more than six million American women entered the work force, often doing what was formerly considered "man's work" (pretty much anything besides teaching and secretarial work). When the war was over and the men came home, most women did as they were expected—they gave the men back their jobs and returned to their domestic duties.

Imagine a woman in the 1940s who goes to work at an aircraft factory during the war. This is her first work outside the home, and, after the war, she gives up that job and returns to her domestic duties. How do you think her experience in the workplace might have changed the way she viewed herself and her role in the world?

★ Equal Pay for Equal Work ★

In 1860, women workers at a shoe-factory in Lynn, Massachusetts, earned one dollar a week while men earned three dollars a week. To this day, the average salary for men is higher than for women.

Why do you believe women have historically been paid less than men? Do you think this will ever change? If so, tell how. If not, tell why not.

★ A Woman President? ★

Margaret Chase Smith (1897–1995) of Maine was the first woman to sit in both the House of Representatives (1940–1949) and the Senate (1949–1973). She ran for president of the United State in 1964.

When do you think a woman will be elected president of the United States? Give reasons for your answer. Is there a woman you would like to see elected president? If so, who is she, and why do you think she should be president?

The Last 50 Years

★ The Kennedy-Nixon Debate ★

On September 26, 1960, Richard F. Nixon (1913–1994) and John F. Kennedy (1917–1963) participated in the first televised debate in presidential campaign history. The debate came at a bad time for Nixon, who was just getting over a serious illness and looked awful. Kennedy, on the other hand, appeared to be the picture of health. Who won the debate? Radio listeners thought there was no clear winner. Television viewers, however, named Kennedy the clear winner.

What do the results of this debate say about appearances? Do you think appearances are important? Should they be? Is it possible for people to get past appearances when making a choice such as who to elect for president? Explain.

★ What Can You Do for Your Country? ★

In his 1961 inaugural address, President John F. Kennedy (1917–1963) said, "Ask not what your country can do for you— ask what you can do for your country."

How well do you think most people follow Kennedy's advice? What are some things people ask the country to do for them? What are some things people can do for their country?

★ Diem's Death ★

Unhappy with South Vietnam's president, Ngo Dinh Diem, President John F. Kennedy (1917–1963) secretly allowed the Central Intelligence Agency (CIA) to plot Diem's murder. Diem's death on November 1, 1963, only made the South Vietnamese government more unstable, however, and encouraged North Vietnamese communists to escalate the war against their southern neighbor.

When, if ever, is it right for the leader of one country to be involved in the murder of the leader of another country?

★ The Draft ★

As the United States increased its involvement in the Vietnam War, President Lyndon B. Johnson (1903–1973) relied on the Selective Service system—the draft—to supply troops. Many well-off young men avoided the draft by enrolling in college. (Student draft deferments, as they were called, were ended in December 1969.) As a result, many of the young men who were sent to Vietnam were from less-well-off families.

Who, if anyone, do you think should be allowed to get out of being drafted? How was the policy of student deferment used during the Vietnam War unfair to less-well-off young men? If you were a male of draft age during the Vietnam War, would you have enrolled in college to avoid the draft? Explain why or why not.

★ "Living Room War" ★

Television brought the Vietnam War directly into the homes of United States citizens. For the first time, people watched a war on the nightly news.

How is seeing a war on television different from reading about it in the newspaper or hearing about it on the radio? How does this difference affect people?

★ The Pentagon Papers ★

The Pentagon Papers, which *The New York Times* printed in 1971, showed that the United States was much more involved in the Vietnam War than the president ever told Congress and the American people. The revelations of the Pentagon Papers further eroded support for the war.

Is the president obligated to tell Congress and the American people everything about the United States' military involvement? Give reasons to support your answer.

★ Unwelcome Heroes ★

After the war, returning Vietnam veterans did not get the welcome the United States usually shows its war heroes. These veterans suffered as much as previous war veterans, but because the war had been unpopular, they were ignored or criticized for the role they played in it.

Tell whether or not it was fair to treat Vietnam veterans poorly when they returned from the Vietnam War. How should these men and women have been treated upon their return? Why do you suppose it was so hard for many people to treat them in a positive manner?

★ Man on the Moon ★

On July 10, 1969, American astronauts Neil Armstrong and Edwin Aldrin, Jr., became the first men to set foot on the moon. Neil Armstrong, hopping off the ladder of the lunar module *Eagle* onto the lunar surface, said, "That's one small step for man, and one giant leap for mankind."

Explain what Armstrong meant? Do you agree or disagree? Tell why.

★ Watergate ★

The Watergate scandal started as an attempt to sabotage President Richard Nixon's Democratic challengers and ended in an illegal cover-up. On August 9, 1974, facing the threat of impeachment, Nixon (1913–1994) became the first U.S. president ever to resign from office. His successor, Gerald Ford (1913–), later pardoned him.

Do you think Ford should have pardoned Nixon for his involvement in the Watergate scandal? Justify your answer.

★ "Greed Is Good" ★

The business mentality of the 1980s was clearly stated by Ivan Boesky. This Wall Street manipulator told a 1986 graduating class of business students, "Greed is all right, by the way . . . . I think greed is healthy. You can be greedy and still feel good about yourself."

What do you think of Boesky's advice? Is it good for people to be greedy? Why or why not?

★ The Persian Gulf War ★

General H. Norman Schwarzkopf, overall commander of operations in the Gulf War, said, "Any soldier worth his salt should be antiwar. And still there are things worth fighting for."

Do you agree with General Schwarzkopf? If so, what do you think is worth fighting for?